THE POWER OF P'S

BY

DAVID L. WASHINGTON

Retired Fire Chief of Las Vegas Fire & Rescue

Library of Congress Control No: 2012950164

ISBN: 978-0-9762347-8-4

Published by: TJG Management Publishing Services, Inc.

THE POWER OF P'S

The Power of P's

David L. Washington

THE POWER OF P'S

My story of how words with the letter "P" incited strength in my life to get me through my tenure as a man of service in the fire fighting industry. From layman to becoming the first African American Fire Chief of Las Vegas, I share my story with you in hopes to instill within you the power of words with the letter "P"~ David L. Washington

CONTENT

Dedication

I dedicate this writing to women who have and those who continue to greatly influence my life. I describe them each with a word from the most powerful letter of the alphabet – The letter 'P'

(*Italics denote those who have gone home to God)

Eugenia Washington - Passionate/prayerful
Rena Watkins – Prayerful/pushy
Mary Wilson – Proud
Charlotte Cooks – Progressive
Della Smith – Positive
Doris French – Practitioner
Marcia Washington - Prayerful/proud
Georgia Grayson - Proud
Ruby Duncan - Principled/purpose driven
Ella Turner - Proud,
Brenda Williams - Persistent,
Faye Duncan Daniel – Philosophical
Bessie Braggs - Poised
Arlene Jackson - Proud
Jacque Matthews - Polished
Pat Ramos - Proud
Dorothy Smith - Pushy
Linda Willis - Patient
Rose James - Personable
April Washington - Pleasant/potential
Gwen Brown Coleman - Practitioner
Magnolia Kennedy - Poised
Virginia Valentine - Progressive
Angel Washington - Potential/proud
Amber Armogan - Prayerful/potential

Loretta Arrington - Personable
Betsy Fretwell - Pushy
Barbara Jackson - Polished
Sandy Toles - Proud
Claudette Enus - Poised
Debra Ann Washington - Personable
Alma Hewitt - Pushy
Kathy Richardson - Prayerful
Moneta Armstrong - Practitioner
Wendy Ennis - Personable
Rosemary Hall - Peaceful
Alice Key - Passionate
Bonnie Juniel - Pushy
Anna Bailey - Practitioner
Shannon West - Productive
Nedra Armstrong - Pushy/principled
Eva Whaley - Prayerful
Hert Taylor - Personable
Gloria "Pee Wee" Foster - Preacher
Bonnie Hogan - Personable
Julie Murray - Purpose/positive
Ricki Nero - Passionate
Sarann Knight-Preddy - Progressive
Erma Walker - Personable

I honor these aforementioned human beings because of their respective commitment and contribution to making a better world. I honor their words of wisdom shared with me at times when I needed a guiding light of encouragement.

As I express and share the Power of P's, I trust you will have a greater appreciation for why I hold these women in such high esteem.

INTRODUCTION
by DR. DOUG SELBY

In life you meet many people. Some of these people leave a lasting impression on you because they are caring, passionate individuals who have committed to make the world a little better place than how they found it.

David L. Washington is one of those people. In his book, The Power of P's, he shares his philosophy and some of his life experiences that shaped him as a human being. The challenges he faced were real, but his internal and external struggles tell the tale of a man who learned that faith, family and friends should be more important than money, power and prestige.

His journey is one that many of us can relate to but more importantly learn from.

In the last pages of his book he sums up much of his philosophy on life with the simple line "God has placed each of us here at this time to do good by one another".

Wouldn't the world be a much better place if we each remembered this simple statement as we go about our busy days?

Douglas Selby
Las Vegas City Manager 2002 - 2009

Prayer

Prayer gives us a strength that has more power than any man can conceive.

MARK 11:24 - **For this reason I am telling you, whatever you ask for in prayer, believe (trust *and* be confident) that it is granted to you, and you will [get it].**

The very first "P" I feel compelled to express and enlighten you with is my belief in the *Power of Prayer*.

Throughout my lifetime, just as with any other human on this earth, many experiences that life offered, proved to be challenging.

If not for the Power of Prayer and the many people who believe in its strength, my journey through my fire service career would have been much more turbulent.

On many occasions, while out shopping or running errands, people from various walks of life would stop me to say hello. These people would share with me that they were praying for me. Some did not know me personally. They simply felt in their hearts that I was a good person and expressed for that reason alone, I was in their prayers.

I often wondered why a person would pray for me when they only knew about me from what they heard or read about me in the press. Admittedly, some of the stories written were not always the most positive things to read. In the early eighties, one newspaper even suggested that the only reason I was promoted to Fire Administration Officer (staff captain) was simply because I was president of the Professional Black Firefighters of Las Vegas.

Nothing could have been further from the truth. I spent no time attempting to defend my promotion at that point. More important to me was the fact that complete strangers were praying for me and my well being! That is undeniable power!

I say this because no harm came to me even though some attempted to take me down during tenure as fire chief. Mayor Oscar B. Goodman had received anonymous letters suggesting that I be fired. I humbly estimate only 10 to 15% of those letters were based on truth. Yet, once again, prayer saw me through those challenging times, not to mention that Mayor Goodman wasn't one to be pushed around.

The prayer of family and friends is no less significant than those of strangers. I didn't realize it until my wife brought it to my attention right after I officially joined Victory Baptist Church that she and my mother prayed deeply for me on a routine basis. Wow!

In retrospect, in my heart, I knew something was happening in a positive way for me. Many years prior to being appointed Fire Chief, there were a few times that I would drink so heavily that my keys should have been taken and transportation home should have been arranged. I know it was absolutely the collective prayers of family, as well as strangers that kept me safe, not to mention that these prayers also kept safe others whom I could have maimed or killed.

I assure you that if I had gotten a DUI, there would have been no way I would have been offered the position of fire chief for the City of Las Vegas.

Just as important, once I became fire chief, there were many other calls to prayer. People that I have known most or all of my life would call unexpectedly to pray for me *over the telephone* because they believed prayer was a necessity at that particular moment.

Often, after such a call, I would just sit in my office to reflect on my journey. There was a time that I once cried while thanking God for sending Dr. William H. Bob Bailey, a longtime family friend, my way at such difficult times.

Additionally, as I established chief's meetings with supervisory level staff officers of Las Vegas Fire and Rescue, several mentioned that they routinely prayed for me. When a staff member asked if he could pray for me at the end of one of those meetings, my answer was simply - ABSOLUTELY.

During his prayer he asked that our Heavenly Father keep a shield of safety around me as I served the community and members of our department. Ethnicity, gender and age were insignificant. The **power** was in the prayer.

Early in my tenure as fire chief, Monroe and Brenda Williams, close family friends, gave me a gift. It was the book 'Prayer of Jabez' written by Bruce Wilkinson. For those who are not familiar with this book it has to do with Jabez asking God to expand his sphere of influence over others in a positive way.

This brief story comes from 1 Chronicles Chapter 4 Verses 9 and 10. It reads, "Jabez was more honorable than his brethren; and his mother called his name Jabez saying, because I bare him with sorrow. And Jabez called on the God of Israel, saying, 'Oh that thou wouldest bless me indeed, and enlarge my coast, and that thine hand might be with me, and that thou wouldest keep me from evil, that it may not grieve me!' And God granted him that which he requested."

As the new fire chief, I was assured that my sphere of influence had indeed been expanded.

Prayer is one the best gifts we receive. I found and continue to find this to be true. I'm a firm believer that we can all use prayer in our lives to ensure safe passage.

I had a praise team (Pastor Eva Whaley, Marcia Washington, Gloria Burns and Ernest Fountain) that I called upon as I served as Fire Chief for the City of Las Vegas, as well as calling upon my personal Savior. I must tell you that praise team member Pastor Eva Whaley called me many a morning to pray for me prior to the start of my day. Pastor Whaley later became one of three chaplains for Las Vegas Fire & Rescue. Part of those duties included leading prayer for newly promoted personnel at our staff meetings.

As I speak of prayer, I would be remiss if I didn't share with you my wife's personal and spiritual experience that took place while attending a church service. During this particular Sunday service, she was spoken to by the Holy Spirit. In faith, she told me that God told her to tell me I must spend time in prayer, bible study, meditation, and fasting. She went on to inform me that I would indeed become fire chief; moreover, I should be prepared for an onslaught of attacks on my character.

I, a man who was building a relationship with God, had faith in His message to me. I immediately began with early morning prayer which included reading my bible and meditating while fasting at least once or twice a month. I would do a 12 or 24 hour fast each time.

Unsurprisingly, the character attacks started the day our city council voted to ratify my appointment. During the public comment portion of the meeting, our Union President suggested that he was afraid of me and that I was unworthy to serve as fire chief.

My assumption was that he felt that way because of my assertive and *"in your face"* style and approach as a fire training officer. It was also very possible that he was aware of the few occasions during my career that I verbally "lost my cool." I will discuss more about that behavior later.

I continued to pray my own simple daily prayer which is "Dear God please give me strength to do your will as I go about this day - Amen" Very seldom does a day go by that I fail to say that simple prayer to our God.

In sharing this prayer with you, I hope it will encourage you to find faith in the Power of Prayer and use it as you serve others.

Finally, with respect to the Power of Prayer, according to God's Word "Be anxious for nothing, but in everything by prayer and supplication, with thanksgiving, let your requests be made known to God." Philippians 4:6 NKJV

Persistence

"Persistence" is something that we sometimes learn over time.

Throughout our lives there are often times when we feel like quitting and giving up, knowing it's the easy way out. Sometimes we have to see the struggle of others in order to appreciate that our plight isn't so bad after all.

Persistence leads to success. When you are determined to reach your goals and be successful at them, persistence becomes second nature.

With persistence and faith, you ensure that your aspirations will come to fruition. However, that does not mean that you will not encounter trials and tribulations along the way.

As I sought to become Deputy Fire Chief another colleague earned the position. Words cannot describe my disappointment. As such, I really didn't care who knew how upset I was in having been passed over for that particular promotion. In fact, I became quite angry until listening to my wife and several women friends, who basically told me to trust in God and know that He has something else in store for me down the road. It took some time, but their collective counsel began to resonate within me. Little did I know or think it would mean that I would become fire chief a few years later.

God promised us safe passage and not necessarily a smooth journey through life as long as we believe and have faith.

We all have a difficult day or week from time to time and generally it is those tough times that strengthen our character.

When one speaks of being persistent, I was. Once I felt I had what it takes to run a fire department, I took the advice of several mentors and role models and applied for two fire chief positions outside of the city of Las Vegas. Yes, I was persistent. I didn't give it a second thought. I prepared and pushed forward.

It would have been easy to just quit after having been told numerous times that I was not good enough or lacked what it takes to head up a fire department. Somewhere in my archives, I have a couple of Dear John letters to prove I had been turned away. One department was Reno, Nevada another was a small three station department in northern California. But, there was no quitter in me, only short pauses to retool as well as dust off my bruised ego. These mementoes continue to remind me to keep persevering.

I would like to share a poem that was given to me by my mother shortly after I became a chief officer (fire training chief) with Las Vegas Fire Department in 1990.

The poem is framed with a picture of a beautiful sunset overlooking the ocean. I trust that you have seen something similar somewhere during your travels. It hung in my office throughout my tenure as fire chief. When I retired October 2007; I hung it in my home office. It continues to remind me to never quit.

DON'T QUIT
When things go wrong, as they sometimes will,
When the road you're trudging seems all up hill.
When the funds are low and the debts are high
And you want to smile, but you have to sigh.
When care is pressing you down a bit,
Rest if you must, but don't quit.
Life is queer with its twists and turns,
As every one of us sometimes learns,
And many a failure turns about,
When he might have won had he stuck it out;
Don't give up though the pace seems slow,
You may succeed with another blow.
Success is failure turned inside out,
The silver tint of the clouds of doubt,
And you never can tell how close you are,
It may be near when it seems so far,
So stick to the fight when you're hardest hit,
It's when things seen worse,
That you must not quit

Finally, with respect to not quitting, my mother never quit attempting to accomplish goals she set during her God given 74 years on this earth. Case in point, it wasn't until she was in her late forties or early fifties, as I recall, that she completed her General Education Development (GED) certificate which is basically completing high school. As a youngster, she had only completed up to the eighth grade. She needed a GED in order to be accepted into cosmetology school. She didn't let her age hinder her goals.

I can state *unequivocally* that she is where I got the fire in my gut from. Mother had tremendous drive to achieve her goals. She, along with our father, encouraged us all to make something of ourselves. We all miss her presence yet she remains in our hearts and minds.

As most of us realize, one of the easiest things to do is to quit. I encourage each of you to take on the attitude of my mother and many others to never quit. During my fire service career, I have witnessed many folks of all ethnicities, male and female, who gave up, yet were quick to blame others for their inability to keep forging ahead.

I must add that it is also important that one not be afraid to fail. We've all heard or read somewhere the same stories in which a number people have mentioned that they failed many times before achieving what most others perceive as *"overnight success"* happened. Overnight success is a myth. You must be persistent as you journey through life and just like the poem states: "Rest if you must, but don't you quit!"

Peacefulness

Peaceful – Free from strife, violence or commotion

PSALMS 34:14
Depart from evil and do good, seek, inquire for, and crave peace and pursue (go after) it!

"P" peacefulness - Over time I have been able to attain the spirituality that leaves me feeling much calmer than in the past. It was not so long ago that my temper and anger always had me ready to fight at the drop of a hat.

I believe that God's desire is that the violence stop and be replaced with peace. There were times in my life when there were no peaceful thoughts, whatsoever, and I would only think vindictive thoughts of how to get even with someone for what I considered to be a major challenge to my manhood.

We have all been there from time to time. Over the course of my life, like some of you, I have been involved in bar fights, street fights and I was even shot in the face.

A dear sister friend, Faye Daniel, once told my wife that I was just a violent person for no particular reason. I figured it was a part of my wild crazy character for whatever God given reason – DNA.

After a level of maturity, which in my case only came with time (age), I learned to not be so serious about the minor/major issues. I can recall several times during my life I would go looking for someone to hurt because of what someone told me they said about me. At the time, I lacked the ability to control my emotions. Instead, I was intent on getting even.

Early in my career it was nothing for me to drive to a fire station to confront one of my colleagues because of what someone told me they had said about me. I would be furious with anger. The only way I could calm myself was to seek someone out and set them straight. Now, at this stage of my life, I realize it really doesn't matter what others say about you if you know who you are and what you represent.

People and the statements they make don't control you, only you do! I know for sure there are times when taking care of yourself and/or your family is a necessity and every man who is worth a grain of salt would want to take proper action in honor of family. In other words, if someone disrespected your spouse or child you may want to deal with them in no uncertain terms. But now, more times than not, I depend on one of my philosophies in life which is – many people talked negatively of Jesus Christ, so who am I to think no one will talk about or disrespect me?

One should maintain peaceful thoughts as God's people while realizing there is a time for war and certainly for peace. I will close out this part with an example of how God can work on you and ensure that you act in a peaceful way.

While serving as interim Fire Chief one of my colleagues came to my office ranting and raving about something he felt that I had done to wrong him. I tried to reason with him and asked that he chill out, but to no avail. I calmly rose from my seat and told him to get his m...... f...... ass out of my office and to never come back until he could be more respectful.

"So…what?" you might wonder. Well, in hindsight I can tell you that God was with me that day. As I mentioned earlier, in my youthful years, I would not hesitate to fight if I was disrespected in any way. In years past there would have been a fight and I would have lost my job and would not have become fire chief. Seek peacefulness from God through prayer and it will come to you. There is nothing you can do but go along with His program - period.

As I reflect, I still can't believe how peaceful and calm I was that day. With maturity comes wisdom and mental growth. It's such a grand thing to be calm and peaceful versus resorting to physical violence or verbal confrontations. I would be remiss if I didn't inform you that the colleague mentioned earlier later became a big supporter throughout my tenure.

"The Lord will fight for you, and you shall hold your peace and remain at rest" (Exodus 14:14 AMP)

Priorities

Priorities-Establishing your priorities are essential to your success

Priorities - During our journey through life many of us have issues with establishing priorities. Knowing how to prioritize projects as well as other matters in your life is one of the keys to making life a lot less stressful. Learning what should take precedence in your life is something that we all come face to face with. When there is no balance and working order that can be applied to your daily living, it can become chaotic. Living in chaos is certainly a recipe for disaster.

Some things must take precedence over others. Remaining true to myself and my beliefs has allowed me to prioritize my life in such a way that suits me. My priorities fall in line as follows: First and foremost, honor God. My family is second, while maintaining a healthy relationship with friends and lastly followed by the business and social aspects of my life.

The prior statements are my gut feelings about God and family. Yet, I have found through bible study that the three highest priorities in your life should be as follows: first in your marriage, your commitment is to Christ, secondly, commitment to your spouse, thirdly your commitment to your children, should you have any and lastly is your work/career.

I know that one of the keys to success is commitment. Without commitment you are undoubtedly doomed to fail. Know that your commitment goes far beyond you. *Be willing to assist others.*

I have spent much of my adult life assisting others through various charitable organizations. Yet I learned to pick and choose not only the number but the types of boards and committees I involve myself with. In my case they generally have to do with our youth. Setting goals is extremely important. However, without establishing priorities, those goals, no matter how great, will more than likely fail to materialize.

While preparing myself to compete for Fire Chief, I had to establish study time as a top priority. Study time ensured that I would be ready to present my knowledge, skills and abilities during any assessment center or examination oral process.

We must prioritize continuously if we are to compete at the highest level. Some of my fellow candidates and fire service colleagues marginalized me for various reasons, even suggesting that I was too militant. I was told that I was *'too Black'* to be allowed to serve as fire chief for our department.

Do you recall when baseball caps with an X on the front were a fad? My children bought me several. Well some folks associated it with Malcolm X. Another officer who happened to be Black told me that I would never become fire chief due to my lack of operations (field) experience. Later he would be one of the first to congratulate me.

I felt from the personal priorities that I set, success in any endeavor would ultimately come, in spite of the opposition of others. Yet, it would have to do with God's will as He sent messages to me through others about what would be most important for me to do in my preparation.

Prayer, meditation, bible study and fasting would be the cornerstone priorities of preparation!

Principles

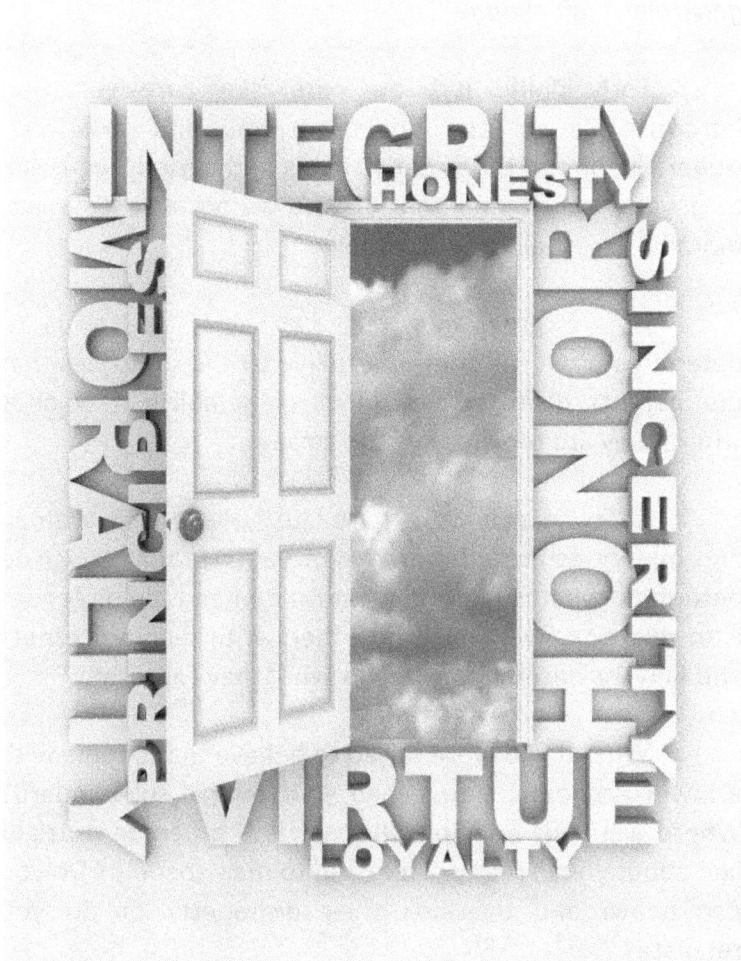

Principles - Guiding sense of the requirements and obligations of right conduct

Your principles are something you live by and they generally don't change

Early in life, it is our parents or caregivers that introduce us to our original beliefs and principles. Generally, during those early stages and periods we begin to develop our foundation for who we are as individuals; morally, personally and spiritually.

As we grow into our own, it is up to us to determine if we will continue to live by the principles that our parents have instilled in us or establish new ones where they are too weak or too strong.

Suppose you were raised to believe that women and minorities are inferior. When you are old enough to determine what is fair and what isn't when race or gender is in question, will you treat others with dignity, respect and fairness based upon who or what they represent?

What if you were raised to believe that people with a lower economic status than your own is substandard? Where will your principles lie? What if a person outright lied about you in many places and to many people? Do you rise above and overlook their dishonesty or do you retaliate?

Challenges to your life principles often present themselves in various ways. There may be times when someone will ask you to put aside your principles and vote with them or make a selection based on that which has no merit. Will you violate your principles and do something that goes totally against everything that you stand for to please someone else?

Your principles represent who you are as a person and you shouldn't allow an effort of persuasion by anyone to change your position relative to any issue. I trust that you have come across folks who would abandon their principles because pressure is brought to bear. On more than one occasion pressure tactics against me included statements to the press that were skewed in order to pressure me to change my position on certain issues. It's really amazing how people will attempt to make you feel as though you are doing something wrong because you're not doing what *they* think you should do or handling things as they would.

No matter what, be true to yourself and your beliefs! When it is all said and done people will respect you more rather than less. One extremely principle-oriented person I was able to emulate over the years is Welfare Rights advocate Ms. Ruby Duncan. For years she took on the federal, state and local governments, as well as big businesses, i.e. Las Vegas strip hotel owners. Ms. Ruby stuck to her guns no matter what others may have thought and when it was all said and done she was able to get things done her way. Ms. Ruby Duncan is a living legend. She encouraged me, along with many other young men and women from our Westside Community of Las Vegas, to be all we could be. She reminds us not to forget to give back to our community.

"PRINCIPLES ARE ONLY GOOD IF YOU CAN STICK TO THEM EVEN WHEN IT'S NOT CONVENIENT" – Unknown

Practice

Practice – something we do to become better at what you are capable of doing.

Generally speaking, everyone would like to be very good at whatever it is they do. We all wish to put forth our absolute best effort. The way we practice, in many respects, reveals who we are as fellow human beings and may also be indicative as to how we will react under pressure. As I prepared myself for the position of fire chief, I spent time practicing what I was going to say during the interview process. I never had any intentions of going in sounding like a programmed robot during the interview process, but I knew that I had to spend a certain amount of time preparing.

During the course of practicing, normally my wife would assist me, but for some reason my wife seemed to take a lackadaisical attitude about drilling me with questions as she had done during other promotional preparation processes. I found myself getting upset because I knew how important practicing is. When she finally did help me, she posed tough questions which made a very discernible difference in my overall confidence. While it didn't make me perfect, I sure felt good about myself.

I have spoken to a great number of people who have admitted that they spent little or no time preparing for a given testing selection process. I will include myself as well. I recall once early in my career taking the fire captain's exam only *hoping* to pass. I say hoping because I had only spent about two weeks preparing only to fall on my face with a score of 68. I was very upset about my poor performance. It was my wife, however, who asked the simple question, "How long did you practice and prepare?" The light went off in my head when I said two weeks. It is essential that one understands that when preparation meets opportunity, there is a much greater chance for success. I imagine we have all heard more than one friend or colleague say, *"I wish I had put in more time practicing to prepare myself for that examination process."*

The fire service, as a profession, is known for continuous drilling. Practice is the reputation fire service professionals are known for. It helps them to be efficient when they encounter a myriad of emergencies. Certainly fire service workers do not hold the corner on the need to practice, athletes are another great example. Any time you see or read stories about the great ones - from boxers, to golfers to basketball players - they all have a common thread as to why they excel. It's the tremendous number of hours they spend practicing their respective crafts. So let's *all* practice and practice some more *until* practicing becomes a way of life.

Passion

Passion - A feeling of enthusiasm deep within your soul for something or someone, yet, not in a lustful way.

You should have passion about whatever you choose to do and do it with all your heart and soul. To be passionate is to have that burning drive to love doing something so much that you would do it for free, we've all heard that stated before. Yet, we can all cite examples where we have witnessed those who lack passion and drive. Many times a great number of people spend a life time without ever knowing their life's passion. As such they go through life being unhappy and all the while wondering why. With respect to those who are passionate about their work, don't you just love being around them? I don't spend too much time staying inside some box or another that someone else might suggest. I was quite passionate about my work in the fire service during my 33 year career. Yet you must still be wise to seek that something that you have a passion to do. Go for it! Be a person of honor as you do so!

Mrs. Ella Turner's Poem (My God Mother)
Man of Honor ~ Fire Chief, Dave Washington

For the many years, you've worked and served,
My son you are getting only what you deserve.
I thank God for using you in this profession and place.
For truly there's no greater task than risking your life
 on a daily pace.
For your leadership skills, I applaud you for leading well.
You've given me pride and a good story to tell.
The first African American to hold the title you've acquired,
Las Vegas, Dave Washington is a man truly to be admired
May God keep you and bless you. Congratulations! Love, Mama

Like my mother, my Godmother was very proud of me and she would brag about me to all of her friends. (Can't you tell by the poem?) But, I was equally as proud of her, a single parent for many years who raised five strong females in the city of Detroit, Michigan.

She had tremendous passion in raising my God-sisters. She ensured that they all completed high school. You might wonder why I feel that Mrs. Ella Turner was so passionate in rearing the girls as she did. It was the way she described the attention she gave to their well being. Another of her passions was playing the piano and boy could she play! She played for several churches in the city of Detroit.

As I complete my thoughts regarding passion, particularly as it relates to my journey on the path to becoming fire chief, I served in at least eight other positions. Most important is the fact that once I lost my passion for a given position, I would seek out something that would reignite that burning drive or passion. Then, I went after it!

Prosperity

Prosperity – A successful flourishing especially in a financial aspect; Good fortune!

PSALMS 118:25
Save now, we beseech You, O Lord; send now prosperity, O Lord, we beseech you, and give to us success!

God wishes prosperity for all who are believers in His word.

I certainly believe this to be factual by virtue of my own example. While seeking to ensure that members of my senior staff were properly compensated for the tremendous work that they continuously produced for our city and its residents, the City of Las Vegas management gave me a substantial raise without my having to ask. I simply wanted their continued support. Unbeknownst to me, not only did I have their support, I also had earned their *respect*. In many difficult times, city management, whom I reported to, had my back. Today, I remain humble and appreciative.

Honestly, I believe, without question, it was God's will that I was better compensated for my service to others. My wife and I have been tithing for many years and God has blessed us for doing so. While more money is nice, it's important for me to note that having many great friends and family makes me very rich and indeed blessed.

I have witnessed how God allowed people to prosper in ways of finance and career success yet they failed to share, therefore, never seemed happy with their lives. So again, do prosper as God would have us do, but do not forget about others along the way.

As such Marcia and I have not only given to our church but also to local and national charities as well *because* we know that God has allowed us to prosper. If you take a look, many of our fellow citizens have done equally as much in assisting those who are less fortunate than we are.

Prosperity doesn't mean one must have all the money to be considered worthy or successful. I trust that we all know people who don't have a great deal of money yet they are prosperous. To have great health is another example of prosperity but one of the greatest examples of prosperity is the love of God and Family!

"People of the Letter P"

Dave, Mike McCoy, Nick Sandoval, Richard Steele, George Knapp

**Clark County School District Paybac Program
Classroom session**

Mayor Oscar Goodman and David L. Washington

Dr. Carl Holmes, Executive Director of Executive Development
Institute (EDI) and David L. Washington, Graduate

Eugenia Washington-White (my mother)

Ella Turner – (Godmother) and David L. Washington

Kathy Richardson and Alma Hewitt (my sisters)

The Washingtons
Vernon, Amber, Marcia, Dave, April and Angel

The Grandchildren

**From the top to right - Destiny and Chris
Center row left to right – David, Marcia (wife) David L.
Washington, Mekiyah
Bottom row left to right – Amari, Kasara, KJ**

Proud Grandpa with Kiran and with Kyson

My God sisters with my wife

(Left to right) Melanise Jones, Kathy Burns, Marcia (wife), Jackie Threats and Sylvia Copeland

Purpose

Purpose – Goal, Intended or desired result

ROMANS 8:28 - We are assured and know that [God being a partner in their labor] all things work together and are [filling into a plan] for good to and for those who love God and are called according to [His] design and purpose.

Purpose gives one focus

Living a life with purpose is such a tremendous blessing from God. However, many folks never seem to gain their individual focus. Sometimes finding your purpose in life has absolutely nothing to do with how much money one earns. Often, more times than not, it has to do with serving others and money has no bearing on your personal commitment to that cause at all, period. When you realize or know your purpose the work you involve yourself in will become your away of life. It will be so rewarding to your spirit and person. Many times the message about your purpose God sends through others. Sure, I realize you could ask what does God have to do with it? My answer is **EVERYTHING!** However, you must learn to recognize when a message to you is being conveyed. I had several people tell me that they had dreamed about me and that they saw my purpose as I did which was to lead our department to this next level of greatness.

This is a very inspiring passage:

"Your vision becomes clear when you look inside your heart. Who looks outside, dreams. Who looks inside, awakens." - *Carl Jung*

Specifically speaking when we awaken we begin to open ourselves up to what it is that God wishes us to do. No, I am not a scientist, but I have very strong feelings about how I believe we can accomplish much if we just lend greater focus to our God given purpose. Someone who comes to mind, as I think about the word purpose and knowing yours, is a personal friend Ms. Julie Murray.

Julie is such a positive being. I believe that she was born for the strict purpose of assisting others to find their organizational way particularly as it relates to raising funds. Andre Agassi Preparatory Academy and Three Square Food Bank has been tremendously successful due in part to Julie's work. She has brought not only commitment but focused purpose to her efforts relative to all that she is involved with. Additionally, Julie and another dear friend Jacqueline Matthews assisted me in establishing the Las Vegas Fire & Rescue Foundation. This foundation is still in existence today and its primary purpose is to help people who have gone through some type of disaster and are without funds to make it through the night. Knowing your purpose and functioning within that realm will ensure that others will be helped.

I recommend that you consider reading "The Purpose Driven Life" by Rick Warren and "The Spirit of Leadership" by Dr. Myles Munroe. These are excellent books that cover purpose from a biblical perspective.

Possibilities

Possibilities – When you believe anything is achievable

Live your life to its fullest potential because it is filled with many infinite possibilities. To move possibilities we must take internal and external action otherwise we can count on becoming stagnant in our efforts. From an internal perspective, we must search within ourselves and seek a spiritual connection. To assist with my internal well being, I have spent more time studying the Bible. In taking this journey of self discovery, I suggest determining goals and desires with respect to the possible thing(s) you might choose to do. More times than not, people will assist you in moving forward toward making those possibilities a reality. Take this book as an example. Once family, friends and colleagues learned that I was interested in writing this book, they gave me continuous encouragement. Those were some of the same people who encouraged me to seek the position of fire chief - more about that later. Brenda Williams, in particular, pushed me constantly to write. Encouragement is powerful.

Another quote I find greatly inspirational is:

To accomplish great things we must not only act, but also dream; not only plan, but also believe. - Anatole France.

Many times, I have witnessed people who have stopped believing in what is possible in their lives. They allow the negative statements and baggage of others to weigh them down and slow themselves into total non-action. With faith anything is possible, my friend. As we go about our lives, it is important to observe and seek the examples of other people. Often we allow ourselves to think that we can't do or complete a goal because we got knocked down the first or second time we attempted to accomplish a major goal.

Remember all things are possible even though one must sometimes refocus.

Examples of support are all around us from where we work, play, attend church and the list goes on. Take the time to talk with these individuals. There are stories to be heard, moreover, examples to follow such as these:

A. Robert Demmons, former Fire Chief of San Francisco Fire Department, consistently talked to me about the talent he felt I had in terms of skill, knowledge and ability to become fire chief for a deserving city. I also helped Chief Demmons, as lower ranking officer and President of the Black Firefighters' Association, take on the City of San Francisco over the issue of discrimination. He was an inspiration to me and many others in the fire service.

B. Hershel Clady former Assistant Fire Chief with Los Angeles County Fire Department, like Bob he always encouraged me about the possibilities within the fire service whether you become fire chief or not makes things happen from where you are,

C. Chief Al Nero and Chief John Ryan were two colleagues who pointed me in different directions about leaving my comfort zone and pursuing what was possible outside the city of Las Vegas. Even though I didn't have success, these two individuals were there to teach me about possibilities that exist outside the boundaries of Las Vegas Fire Department.

The point is that sometimes it takes someone else and their encouragement to give us a "push" in the right direction of many possibilities and opportunities.

Poise

Poise – Staying cool, calm and collected while your personal character is under fire

To be poised is to have great discipline and the confidence to maintain coolness about you during very stressful and difficult times. I would be disingenuous if gave the impression that I have been 100% poised throughout my adult life.

However, it is without question that I can look you directly in the eyes and tell you that I'm much more poised at this stage of my life. It has taken many years to get to this point. It doesn't matter about the difficulties I have faced during my personal journey, I am proud of me. God is good. After over five years of retirement from Las Vegas Fire & Rescue, I was required to do a deposition regarding charges of racial discrimination brought by a former executive level officer. To say that I'm sorely disappointed is an understatement, yet as I mentioned earlier, God is good and it is my faith that will keep me poised when the court case takes place. I know from a previous experience in federal court that I will be able to speak in more detail after the trial occurs.

However, I can speak about that previous case in which I was also charged with discrimination by a member of my staff. I was boiling with anger while sitting in that federal courtroom. My attorney reminded me tactfully that I must be cool. To have someone sit before a court and suggest that you didn't promote them because of their religion was painful. It took all that I could muster to maintain my poise and not blurt out that such a statement was a blatant lie.

God seemed to be with me throughout three and a half days of testimony. When it was all said and done I along with the City of Las Vegas was found not guilty of the charges.

During many years of my teenage and adult life I was viewed as a hot head and with good reason. Yet I can tell you that I learned some of what it takes to remain poised by observing others.

My aunt, Magnolia, has always demonstrated great poise and composure in handling matters in difficult or trying situations, while others including me would be somewhat shaky. Another woman of poise is a former colleague, Claudette Enus. She has always remained cool, calm and extremely poised while under vicious attacks from labor union leaders. So even I was able to learn from others and put that better behavior of poise to work in my own private and professional life.

(As I was making the final revisions for this book, during the week of August 6-10, 2012, I had to testify on behalf of myself and the City of Las Vegas in a different trial. The trial was based on a complaint filed by an individual suggesting that I racially discriminated against him. The verdict was in favor of the plaintiff and I am troubled and disheartened by the judgment. I do not engage in discriminatory behaviors or practices and never will. I frown upon anyone who does. I've gone through many federally mandated training sessions and I know better than to support such behavior. Again, to say that I'm truly pained by the finding is an understatement, primarily due to the many lies that were told to the court. However, I will thoroughly share more in detail in my memoirs, which have yet to be written.)

Procrastination

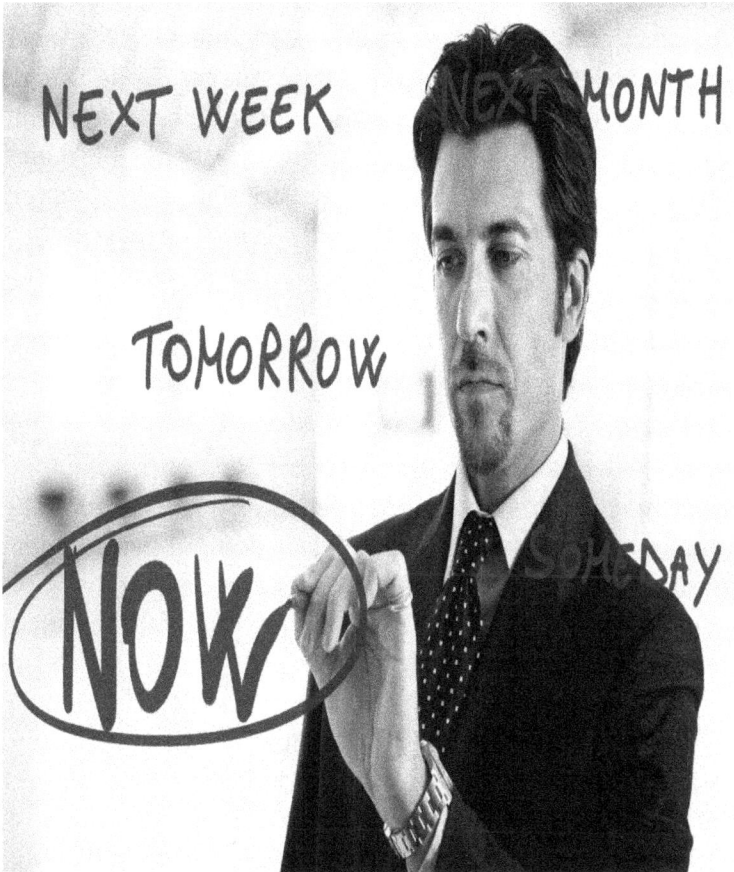

Procrastination – It has stopped many a man and /or woman right in their progressive tracks…..

I wish I was personally above that known human trait of procrastination; however, once again I must share a very personal commitment that I made to two very caring individuals. These people believed in my ability to successfully lead the Las Vegas Fire & Rescue as I was named interim Fire Chief. Eventually, I was appointed to the position. Those two people were the City Manager, Virginia Valentine and Deputy City Manager, Doug Selby. I recall during my promotional interview being asked what was I going to do with respect to the fact that I lacked a bachelor's degree. My answer was to pledge to complete my bachelor's degree. During my tenure, I successfully completed a number of classes towards accomplishing that goal, but I have yet to fulfill my commitment. Being a man of my word, like my father taught me to be, I'm intent on keeping my word some day.

As we know, to *procrastinate is to postpone doing something, even more so postponing as a regular practice.* That is exactly what I found myself doing. I would speak often about registering for a college course or two, yet when it was all said and done, I would fail to follow through.

It's pretty common for people to talk about doing something but become hesitant in following through with the process. It seems to be a human condition to procrastinate. We should condition ourselves as the Nike slogan suggest and *"JUST DO IT"*.

As the old saying goes "your word is your bond". It should be important for us to move ahead and get things done versus postponing our goals.

Pain

Pain-It's that hurt we as people have felt many times during our life's journey.

I would be remiss if, while writing about many of my personal experiences, I didn't address the sometimes dreaded matter called pain. Sometimes that pain is physical other times it's more mental. The more simple form would be physical pain such as receiving a spanking as a child. Like many of you, I'm a better person today because of those lickings I got from my parents, relatives and friends.

Also on the physical level have you ever accidently caused someone that you love pain? There is an incident that I have relived many times. My grandson, David II, was with me while I was working on my truck and I accidentally slammed the door on his finger. The point I want to make is while in deep pain he hugged me with love yet I had caused him pain. Thank God it was determined not to be broken. Nevertheless, I felt great emotional pain because I had hurt my little road dog. To intentionally inflict pain on anyone, let alone a child, is a terrible thing. I still wonder how adults, whom we read or hear about all too often, could hurt any child. Sadly, in a world full of joy, there is so much pain... unintentional, as well as deliberate.

The more complex pain is the psychological pain, in some instances caused by ourselves, because one may fail to follow through. Moreover, that pain could also be due to the loss of a loved one. I recall my dear friend, Hershel Clady, telling me he knew how I felt after losing my mother; however, within seconds after making that statement, he reversed himself. He then told me that he could only imagine how I must feel because at the time his mother was still alive.

I have a few rhetorical questions for you. As a leader have you ever had to deal with the pain of losing an employee to the ravages of cancer? Have you had to oversee what's referred to as a line of duty funeral service? Have you ever had to visit the family of a deceased fellow employee? And lastly, have you ever had to visit a fellow employee who will never walk again due to a serious job related injury? There is no doubt those are matters of pain at the highest level for one to deal with. However, no matter the type of pain we have or will experience, there is an old saying "God will not put any more on any of us than we can bear." Yet once again that's not to say you will not feel pain in many ways.

Planning

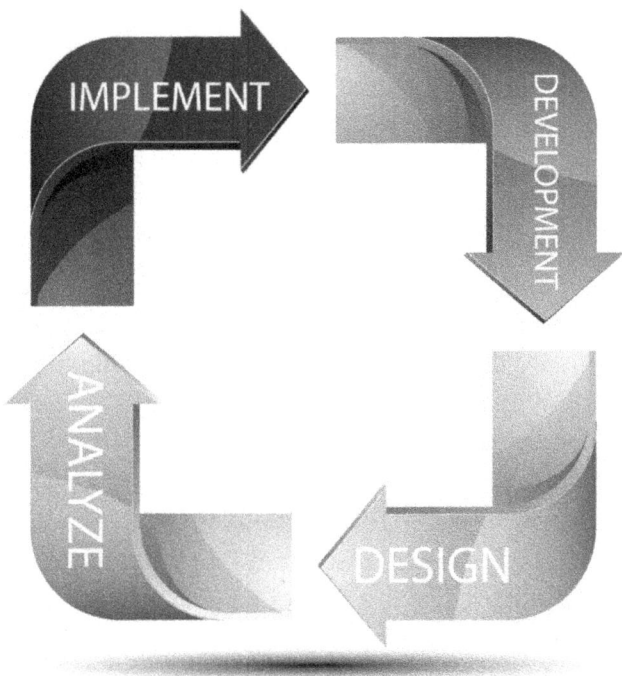

Planning - As the old saying goes, "If you fail to plan you plan to fail."

Not only in our professional lives, but also in our personal lives we have got to establish a plan in order to achieve your desired goals.

Many times we can start out with the best laid plan yet never follow it completely. That isn't a bad thing at all because you at least had some idea of where you were attempting to go.

To be perfectly honest my initial goal was to become a deputy fire chief. This was frankly because in the mid-seventies, when I was hired by Las Vegas Fire Department, discrimination was quite dominant in our department's culture.

In fact, a deceased colleague Fredrick Miles Jameson and I planned for him to become chief and myself deputy. As time passed, discrimination and racism became less of a factor in the selection of officers primarily because of the efforts of the Professional Black Fire Fighters' of Las Vegas not to mention the NAACP.

With those changes in place, I began to rewrite my plan which put *me* in the top job. The plan included seeking out mentors like Monroe Williams (Fire Captain Retired) and Larry Powell (Assistant Fire Chief Retired) Carl Holmes (Assistant Fire Chief Retired) as well as fire service consultant, role models Rex Shelburne Deputy Fire Chief (Retired), John Ryan Fire Chief (Retired).

My plan also included getting, at a minimum, an Associate's degree and attending various training and educational sessions, both in and outside the city. I had to rewrite my plan many times because it was never so perfect that one draft was the complete road map to the success I was able to achieve in my profession. Fire service was never my actual chosen career path to begin with. After serving as a cook in the United States Army, I wanted to be a gourmet chef. However, prior to being discharged from service I took a carpentry apprenticeship that was offered in an effort to prepare one for re-entry into civilian life. George Jackson, a US Marine Veteran and a lifelong friend, worked for the City of Las Vegas and encouraged me to apply for a carpentry apprenticeship program with the city.

When I went to apply, I was informed that I was a day late. The position posted had closed. Yet this young black woman, Dorothy Smith, suggested that I change my plan. I took her advice and applied for a firefighter trainee position on the spot.

Always remember that no plan will sustain forever there will be minor as well as major changes/adjustments from time to time. If you think of life in terms of a business plan, as the business grows, you are constantly adjusting the plan.

My final thought relative to planning is that you should go after something you are passionate about, share your thoughts with others and accept encouragement. I have many friends who have continually pushed me to pursue the unthinkable for some. Yet, we all know that God is the Master Planner who makes all things possible.

Plan while keeping God at the center of what you do.

Progress

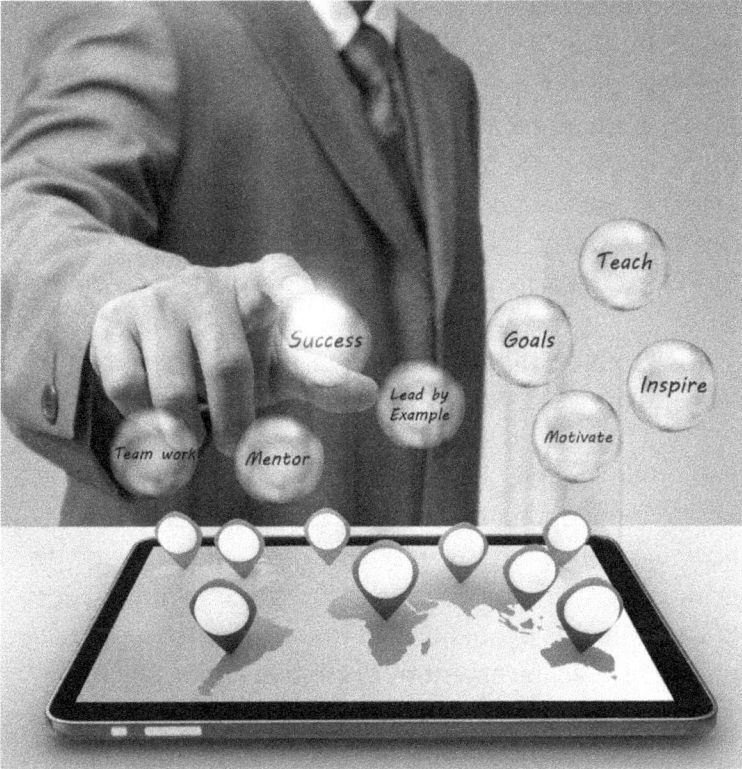

Progress - Simply to move forward towards a particular goal.

In my opinion, my appointment to fire chief isn't so much about the progress of Blacks in our community. I take that stance because it was a greater achievement for the first Blacks to be hired by the department in 1963. James Walker and Monroe Williams were hired because of the work of our local chapter of the NAACP. This was true progress because prior to their being hired, the Las Vegas Fire Department had been a paid professional department for over 21 years without one employee being Black.

Thus, without question, in terms of progress those individuals were what I consider a major breakthrough. This was far more important if one was to compare it to any other major achievement in our community with respect to progress of an ethnic group at that time. It's sad however, that you can't find any mention of their achievement in the archives of the local newspapers. I looked but was unable to find not one sentence about the progressive achievement by these two young Black men.

That particular milestone laid the ground for many Larry Powell, Otis Harris, countless others, including, myself, David L. Washington, to enter into the world of fire services in 1974.

Of importance is to note that Larry Powell retired as an Assistant Fire Chief and was the highest ranking Black officer at that time. Monroe Williams along with William Young were the first two Blacks to become fire captains in the department, continuing to break down barriers. It was the NAACP who pushed open the door for

Blacks and then it was the Black Firefighters of Las Vegas who filed an E.E.O.C complaint that ensured Blacks and other minorities would gain equal access to various promotional opportunities within our fire department like the Powell's, Williams, Washington's and Young's, etc.

Yes progress in the proper context has its place in our history.

With the recent passing of my dear friend Monroe Williams, a true representation of progress, I offer this poem:

"Now Come on Home to Me"
In Loving Memory of Monroe Williams
Written by Angel D. Washington

There's so much to say in so little time
But I promise to do my best
To share some thoughts about a man
That stood above the rest
Not at all in attitude or arrogance
Simply as a man and great friend
Who inspired many and was loved by many
Whose achievements I must commend
Monroe Williams, loving husband to Brenda
And dedicated father of three
To the pride, joys and loves of his heart
Tanya, Kenny and Jolene
A community trendsetter, who paved the way
By tolerating malicious treatment
For blacks to succeed in the Fire Services
Resulting in remarkable achievement
Reaching an inspiring goal as Fire Captain

Before retiring his fire hose
Even after enduring racial discrimination
And premeditated obstacles
A mentor and advisor with great wisdom
His experience was extraordinary
By sharing his knowledge, he saw the potential
Monroe Williams was a true visionary
God sent OUR friend Monroe for a purpose
That purpose was fulfilled and complete
Therefore, God said "Well done, Monroe"
"Now come on home to ME..."

Personable

Personable – Affable, amiable, sociable

It takes various facets of your personality to achieve growth. Refrain from smug and arrogant behaviors. When dealing with others on a personal and professional level, to be likeable is ideal.

As I worked to place myself in a position to be selected as Fire Chief, I never felt above the others, just the better man for the job. In general, one should never become so big in their mind that they are above or better than those around them. I mentioned earlier how I opened my door to supervisory level personnel each year. Just because we become the big man on the block we should not cut ourselves off from those people we work with. I made it a point not to make a person feel small or less than anyone else.

Everyone deserves to be respected as a fellow human being, particularly if they came before us because they had gotten in some type of trouble. I was far from being the model employee. I was arrested several times during the early days of my career. As I served, I would ensure that people felt that I was approachable.

This behavior was especially important when I acted as Fire Chief. I was informed by a fellow director that he and his team members were praying that I get promoted to the position of fire chief. He explained to me that I carried myself with decency and respect for myself and others where one of my competitors would attend directors' meetings and fail to speak to others during his tenure as acting fire chief. He surmised that the gold badge that he wore made him somehow feel bigger than the folks he was competing to serve with. In closing, it just doesn't matter your rank or position within an organization. You will ultimately be judged on your character.

Proud/Pride

Proud - Feeling pleasure or satisfaction over something regarded as highly honorable or creditable to oneself.

Pride – The state or feeling of being proud.

Proud is such a great way to be. I have always considered myself to be a proud man. Having the ability to exercise humility, while having self-pride, is a great quality. I've never been afraid to state that I am an American citizen who happens to have been born Black by God's grace. I'm proud of who and what I am. I'm proud of who I was and who I've become. Yet, while I am proud of who I am, some people have an issue with my ability to be comfortable in the skin I'm in. Being proud allows one to stand for what they believe in, *without fear*. Some people are unable to possess that same self-pride. It was quite obvious when I was preparing myself to seek the position of fire chief.

During the period of time that I was serving as interim fire chief, I met with approximately 40 to 50 members of our staff, from uniform to civilian personnel, for the purpose of gaining incite on how they individually viewed our fire department. Along with the information I received, I gained a lot of knowledge from these colleagues from which I developed my plan. I did this while my fellow candidates for the fire chief position failed to do the same. I felt as though they were too proud to reach out to staff members throughout the organization.

I'm a firm believer that, if you are going to lead others, you must also be willing to reach out to them for opinions as well as ideas. The people want to be heard and they should be.

With respect to pride, I was told by a couple of colleagues that I would never be selected for fire chief because I was too racial and militant. I was surprised that anyone would consider my Blackness as an obstacle. I stand by the notion that we should all conduct ourselves with pride that is not boastful as we walk this earth.

Patience

Patience – Quiet, steady perseverance

Patience - Simply slow down and let some things come to you in God's time.

I am often reminded by my wife Marcia and our youngest daughter, Amber, that I don't have enough patience.

When one writes about their journey, it's extremely important to be honest with one's self and others whom you care about enough that you wish to inspire them through words.

As a career planning instructor, I encourage others to be patient when seeking that promotion. Without patience you can easily lose focus on achieving the position that you are seeking.

I mentioned earlier how upset I was when I didn't get promoted at the time I felt I should have. There are other examples of how I have been more hurried than waiting patiently such as when someone is attempting to share a story or event with me. Little do most folks know, I love the reader's digest version of a story. What I mean is the short description of an event or story is what I prefer when someone is explaining something to me. I would be less than truthful if I didn't inform all that I still struggle in this area to this day. My golf game as high handicapper is a reflection of a lack of patience. I firmly believe that when I begin to show greater patience even my golf game will become markedly better.

Patience is a virtue that we all have however, some of us have to reach deep within to find it and properly channel ourselves to ensure we slow down.

Potential

Potential – Possibility, personal development

The Final P-Potential-This is something that God gives us all

The question is what do we do with it? For the last twenty (20) years, I have participated as an Instructor at the Carl Holmes Executive Development Institute (EDI). Our institute has been housed at several historical Black colleges. I must name them because I believe they have the great potential to inspire Black youth - Florida A & M University, Dillard University and Clark Atlanta University. More importantly throughout EDI's existence, I have had the opportunity to interact with some of the brightest minds, young and old in the fire service.

One of the key responsibilities given to me by Dr. Carl Holmes is to recognize and inspire the God given talent in each student. More often than not you find that back at home in their respective fire departments they have to deal with many obstacles.

An example is failure by upper management to recognize their individual potential because of their race. As a part of my personal obligation, I do my best to shake and awaken our people to seek, through personal dedication and commitment, their rightful place in the fire service business and that place is in a leadership role.

By leadership role, I am not suggesting that one must be chief of the department to lead. It can and must be done in all areas of life from father, mother, sister, brother to supervisor on your job.

If others can, you surely can as well and God expects us to utilize the talents that we were blessed with.

No excuse will do for your not using your God given talent.

During the journey of my life, there have been many ups and downs. I'm grateful to God for His many blessings.

As I look back on my life, I've had far more ups, than downs. As fellow human beings, we all experience the many challenges of life. In our personal experiences, we must learn to deal with the good as well as the bad in a positive manner. People make judgments and that is a part of life that we must all deal with. I don't believe I need to assure you that the only judge that can evaluate ones character is God.

I retired from the fire services over five years ago. In celebration of my retirement, my family and I decided to host a dinner party for a number of individuals whom we felt had been an inspiration to me throughout my life as well as career. We invited around 85 people that consisted of family members, friends and colleagues.

Unbeknownst to them, I would be the speaker. However, I did let Virginia Valentine (former city manager of Las Vegas) say a few words. It was truly heartwarming to be blessed by the presence of so many great people who enriched my life. As part of this celebration, I asked one of our daughters to write a poem that would capture the essence of my career and what faith, family and friends have meant to me. It is my hope that you will appreciate the poem as much as I do.

My Journey through Faith, Family & Friends
by Angel Washington

*Faith in God had led me here
I know that this was His plan
I put all of my trust in Him
And took His leading hand*

*I followed Him on a journey that
Was so unknown to me
But I knew that trusting Him would lead me
To my destiny*

*A loving family that supported me
No matter the demand
No weapons formed against me shall prosper
My journey is in His hands*

*Behind a strong man there's a strong woman
My wife is truly superb
I couldn't have found a better soul mate
Had I walked the entire earth*

*When facing adversity, my kids stood tall
Like the soldiers that they are
Ready to go to the front line for battle
To face anyone at war*

There was someone else that God included
During our journey together
A group of people who are dear to me
He couldn't have picked them better

He led me to you, all of my friends
Who were supportive during trying times
I thank Him for you all, because we know
Good friends are hard to find

As I vacate my career and move into retirement
My journey has started again
I give all glory and thanks to God first
Then all of my family and friends....

Without question those are powerful words put to paper that truly capture the essence of David Lee Washington, one of God's children.

Much of what I have accomplished in my life's journey has been inspired by others and most importantly the will of God. To be honest those who truly know me will attest to the fact that I don't need much to survive. My faith, family and friends have meant so much to me during my life, I will be forever grateful for the God given opportunity to serve and reach my potential as a fire service professional.

Closing Remarks

I will continue to maintain my simple philosophy in life which is "Live and let live and do all that I can to make positive contributions to our worldwide society". With that said, know that I put God first for it is because of Him that we are here. My family second because more times than not it's for them I work so hard, as well as pray for each of our children that we were blessed to have. The job would be third, just keeping things in proper perspective because when it's gone some may forget about you and the things of a positive nature that you did.

God has placed each of us here at this time to do well by one another. Always mean what you say and say what you mean. In other words don't just talk about it, be about it! I encourage you to serve and serve some more.

Now that I have retired from the fire service, I plan to maintain my - service to others - mindset. I will continue my work with non-profit organizations and finally I will become a substitute mid-school teacher. I wish each reader great success, a lot of grace, peace always, as well as an abundance of love during your life.

Special Thanks

I must personally thank several of my family and friends for assisting me in their own inspiring way to complete this book: Marcia Washington (wife) who helped when I had computer problems. Angel Washington (daughter) who assisted me with editing, April Washington (daughter) she was the second of our daughters to write and have a book published. Valeria Weiner (State Senator) she taught me how to journal and classmate Debra Nelson (Hotel Executive) for urging me to write about my fire service legacy (next book). Doug Selby (Former City Manager) when I informed him about my book he agreed to write an introduction. Brenda Williams (Interim Councilwoman) who routinely asked about my book as well as introduced me to a life coach that I hired. Frances Richards (life coach) she encouraged me to get off my behind and establish a timeline for completion of my draft this book. Frances is a great coach beyond what she encouraged me to do. Finally, I thank Ms. Theresa Gonsalves for her guidance as publisher of my first book. I must admit that she kept me on the straight and narrow; she suggested several changes which at first made no sense to me. However, after a face to face meeting it became crystal clear that she was right.

Once again each of these folks either did or said something to ensure that I would forge ahead and bring the book to fruition. So I do thank you with all my heart.

About the Author

David L. Washington recently retired as fire chief for Las Vegas Fire & Rescue after 33 years of service with the last six years as department director. David guided the department to many major accomplishments with the assistance of what he refers to as an exceptional staff. That staff consisted of people from all walks of life not to mention both civilian and uniform personnel.

With respect to achievements, Las Vegas Fire & Rescue retained our Insurance Services Office (ISO) class one as well as became an accredited agency by the Center for Public Safety Excellence. After attaining these two achievements, it made our department only one of eight in the world to hold these two prestigious certifications at the same time. Once fire chief, he ensured that the safety of our firefighters was a top priority by requiring that all new assistant chiefs become certified safety officers.

They were able to construct six new fire stations and increase the departments overall staffing. David continues to be proud of the fact that they were able to establish the Las Vegas Fire & Rescue Foundation which provides funds in the form of gift cards in $20 increments to responding firefighters to distribute to individuals who are in need due to the destruction of fire or some other emergency.

Another humanitarian initiative David was involved in is the Safe Place program which allows any child under the age of eighteen a safe haven at any of our fire stations if they find themselves under threat by any person. During an exit presentation before the city council, he expressed his exuberance in having been given the opportunity to serve this great community. With regard to his community work,

David continues to be involved in many community organizations such as the National Forum for Black Public Administrators, I Have a Dream Foundation, Camp Anytown, Camp Brotherhood/Sisterhood, Carl Holmes Executive Development Institute, Communities in Schools, New Ventures Certified Development Company, Black Business Council of Nevada and many more.

Finally, David is a 57-year resident of our community who is proud to say he wisely married his high school sweetheart Marcia of 40 years and they have four adult children and nine grand-children. Marcia and I know that we have been blessed to have a great family life and we love all of our children and grand children very much.

The fire service afforded his family to live a middle class life style. They remain grateful to God.

www.ingramcontent.com/pod-product-compliance
Lightning Source LLC
Chambersburg PA
CBHW031604040426

42452CB00006B/408